Beautiful Transformations

Lisa Ann

Published by Lisa Ann, 2023.

While every precaution has been taken in the preparation of this book, the publisher assumes no responsibility for errors or omissions, or for damages resulting from the use of the information contained herein.

BEAUTIFUL TRANSFORMATIONS

First edition. November 20, 2023.

Copyright © 2023 Lisa Ann.

ISBN: 979-8223787860

Written by Lisa Ann.

Table of Contents

I dedicate this book to my family. I love you with all my heart and to my friends that have helped me along the way.

Introduction

My love for writing poetry began when I was in high school. I had a fantastic teacher in English class Named Mrs. Bolone.

Mrs. Bolone tried to open me up to joining a poetry class, I wasn't ready for it at the time although I would write and keep it to myself. Mrs. Bolone passed away many years ago. I can only hope she knows how much she influenced and touched my life.

I married my high school sweetheart and best friend Scott at the age of 19, on December 30th, 1992. Around four years after we married the first of our three children were born—Rebecca, Megan, and our son Scotty. Life wasn't always easy, but we made it work. I will always thank Scott for that.

Just shy of our twenty-seventh wedding anniversary Scott was taken from our lives, it was completely unexpected. Scotty, Megan, and I tried in vain until paramedics got there to try and save his life, it just wasn't meant to be. Scott passed one month after his 47th birthday. We were shocked and devastated beyond belief. I never thought this would happen to us, we were completely unprepared.

I was lost. We were all lost. I did not know how I was going to get through that. Rebecca stepped up at a young age to help. She was my rock, helping to get through the phone calls and funeral arrangements.

I was inconsolable at that moment. I did not want to go on without my best friend. At this point, the only thing that kept me going was our children. Without their support I would not have made it, they were my only reason to keep going, and all the love and kindness of our family and friends helped us through.

Scott would tell me I was strong, but I never believed it. I would always say back to him, "I am strong because of you", he would then say, "you are stronger than you think". I never thought I would be put through such a test to find this out.

After a period, I started to get things figured out. I met some amazing people along the way that helped our family. Some were people I just came across once on this journey and their kind words and insight will always remain with me.

Scott passed away in November 2019. I only had one grief counseling class before the holidays had put everything on hold. Grief counseling is hard to come by when you live in a rural area and then covid shut everything down. My children and I were utterly alone after that. So, I started to write, do little projects around the house, and helped my kids when they needed it (even though they helped me most) to keep busy and get out of my head so much.

Long story short, after starting to piece my life back together, finding a new job after things started to open back up, and finding us a new place to live that was more affordable, I started realizing how strong I was. It was my faith in God, Scott, and my angels protecting and guiding me. I find strength in knowing they are there. It was not, and has not been easy, I will sit and look at how far I have come, and all the blessings that I have been granted, and I know there are always going to be tests and lessons, that's just life, but I know where to find peace through these times.

One of the greatest blessings of all was the birth of our first grandchild Ollie. As happy as I was, I felt a lot of guilt that Scott would never get to watch him grow. I realized then that he would. I know Scott is always watching over and I believe that he handpicked the most perfect little angel to send to us. Ollie is truly a blessing in our lives. Even though Scott is not with us, I know a part of him is in that little boy and the children, we had together. Scott does live on.

It has always been a dream of mine to write a book, so I gathered all my writings from over the years and put them together. Poems to show that even when you think you have no strength left, you do. To believe in a higher power, whatever that may be to you. Even though endings are hard, there are reasons for them, a new beginning. Lessons, good or bad, are lessons learned. You can overcome anything, no matter how big or small. Some things take time and healing, so give yourself that time. Reach for the support of the ones that love you and who you love. This has been hard but also full of many blessings and on my dark days, I reach for those blessings to carry me through.

This has been my journey so far; A beautiful transformation to finding hope and strength. With the love and support of my family and friends, they would hold me when I cried and just sit with me in the quiet. I never would have made it without them, and I thank God every day that they are in my life and believed in me.

The journey will never be easy, life is never going to be perfect because as humans we are not perfect. It's how you apply the lessons you have learned to overcome the problems. And trying to show compassion for those who have not learned their lessons.

I hope this book helps someone find their own strength and power and if it does then I know this was part of my journey in life. Celebrate your life and accomplishments and live to the fullest every day because life is short.

Scott, I know you will be waiting for me when my time comes. Thank you for being a part of my life and for our beautiful family. I will always love you.

Have faith, and strength, show kindness, and help your fellow man. May God bless you all and I wish you the best on your journey through life.

Love and Light

Intense
Tears of Love
Each and Every Day
Dreams
Forever
Seasons
Good and Bad
Lost in your Eyes
Stay
With Love
Thank God

Intense

These feelings are so intense
My breath was taken away
Butterflies in my stomach
To see you every day

These feelings are so intense
It brings me to tears
Never thought of happiness again
I'm happy when you're near

These feelings are so intense
Overwhelming at the least
I feel it deep inside me
Even when you breath

These feelings are so intense
I hope they never leave
I will wrap you in my love
You make me feel complete

Tears of Love

Your hands are strong
Your soft subtle kiss
These are times I will always miss

Your tender touch
Your warm embrace
I always long to see your face

It's been a long time, a couple of years
Too long for me, I burn with fear
And every night I shed a tear

I miss you and I love you
That will always be true
Maybe someday you will feel this way to

My love will grow over time you will see
Maybe for you, it will never be

Just one thought to remember my dear
My love for you grows with every tear

Each and Every Day

You're my candle in the dark
Moonlight in the night
Sunshine in the day
You make my life bright

All that we have been through
All that we do
This one thing I know
I will always be true

I love you more
With each passing day
I will love you forever
Any shape any way

There are many things
That words cannot say
Always remember this
Each and every day

Dreams

In my dreams
I see your face
It's beauty there
Can't be replaced

In my dreams
You take my fears
Push them away
And dry my tears

In my dreams
You are the love
Sent just for me
From heaven above

Forever

Tears of joy, sadness, and laughter
Times with you forever after
Winter, spring, summer, and fall
We'll be together through them all

We take the good
Accept the bad
And all the time we've ever had

Add them up and you will see
Things couldn't be better
For you and me

Seasons

Red leaves
Gold leaves
Green and Brown
Fall is the time
I love having around

Snowflakes
Cold days
Crisp cool air
Winter is time
For family and cheer

Wildlife
Flowers
Lawns turning green
Spring is time
For new life to gleam

Blue skies
White clouds
Long hot days
Summer is time
To go out and play

Good and Bad

For all the things we've ever had
All the good
All the bad

All the time we've ever fought
All the love that could never be bought

During all these times
Our love has remained true

Forever and ever
I will always love you

Lost In Your Eyes

Lost in your eyes
My breath was taken away
You see into my soul
You make my day

Lost in your eyes
I wish I could read
What's on your mind
What you're thinking of me

Lost in your eyes
I see all your pain
I wished I could make it go away

Lost in your eyes
Wishing for the day
I could swim in your love
And just float away

Stay

I was sent here to help you
Just let me in
Open your heart to me
And then we can begin

I will try to guide you through
And help you find your way
I will hold onto your hand
I will always stay

Bringing you in love
Holding you when you're cold
I promise I will be here
Until we grow old

And when our time is through here
We will have to part ways
Just always know you're in my heart
And that is where you'll stay

With Love

I hope you find your path in life
Hope you learn to grow
My hopes for you are always true
I hope that you will know

Just what you always meant to me
And how you've helped me grow
You helped me see just what I want
And where I want to go

These changes have been good for me
I hope you find yours too
I'm wishing you the best in life

With love from me to you

Thank God

I'm feeling light and happy
Blessed every day
I wonder what I've done right
To have you sent my way

I thank God for the strength he's granted me
Protection I have received
My angels for their guidance
I'm finally feeling free

My path was filled with darkness
Now I see the light
I thank God every day
To have you in my life

Grief

Grief
Gods Choice
My Sadness Runs Deep
Shattered Dreams
Crying Rivers
Loneliness
Little Lamb
Confusion
Dying Love
Waves of Emotion
Clipped Wings

Grief

Grief on my mind
It leaves me feeling torn
A stab to my heart
A pain I must mourn

Grief that's never-ending
Grief that always hangs
Grief that's always there
Filling all my days

No words can ever be spoken
To heal unbearable wounds
Only the time it takes
To move on from this gloom

Gods Choice

It was God's choice
To take you away
I cannot understand why
So, I kneel to him and pray
To dry these tears I cry

I pray to God for guidance
Praying to God for help
Pray for God to walk me through
Emotions never felt

To help me through the dark times
Help me see the light
I pray for God to guide me through
This never-ending plight

My Sadness Runs Deep

My sadness runs deep
Like an ocean untamed
A gash from a wound
I always feel pain

My sadness runs deep
Never wants to stop
It ticks away
Like time on a clock

My sadness runs deep
I wish for the day
That it would lighten up
Or just go away

My sadness runs deep
I'm filled with despair
Lost in time
With nobody there

My sadness runs deep
The wounds have healed
A scar remains that now reveals
The depths of my pain a cross I will bear

My Sadness runs deep
Because you're not there

Shattered Dreams

She screams
As she breaks down inside
While her heart
Is cut like a ribbon

She bleeds.
Like a waterfall overflowing
Cries out like a baby
Then all at once
She is peaceful like the dead

The sounds of shattered dreams remain
We see the dark
Feel the pain

Memories of her
Still live as a gleam
Although we all know
She will never be seen

She lives in our hearts
We feel her pain
Lord this world
Will never be the same

Crying Rivers

The tears start rolling down my face
It feels as if there's little space

First the shock then the calm
When I looked you were gone

It's sad to say but you know it's true
A river to an ocean
Is what I've cried for you

Loneliness

The loneliness consumes me
I only think of you
Wishing you were here with me
I'm only feeling blue

You're not here when I wake
Or go to bed at night
The loneliness consumes me
Fills my world with fright

Day by day I'm alone
It never seems to end
I only want to be with you
My beloved friend

I wish to hold your hand
Or look into your eyes
To feel your warm embrace
And dry these tears I've cried

The loneliness consumes me
I will miss you every day
You're always in my heart
And that is where you'll stay

Little Lamb

There was a little lamb
Taken away
Called out by God
To come and play

A life cut short
Only God knows why
We are left empty and begin to cry

Cry out to God with questions
Why was this soul taken away

God answered with one response
It was this little lamb's day

Confusion

The confusion in my head
It keeps me swirling around
I never know what's up
Never know what's down

Never know the truth
Of where your mind is at
Feels like these are games you play
Feels like I'm left back

Back in a world of confusion
Swirling in my head
Feel like I'm alone
Feeling like I am dead

Dying Love

When we were young
We were bold
As we grew old
Our hearts turned cold

Our love was like
A rose in bloom
Now it's old
And full of gloom

We tried to rekindle
That once burning flame
Now that we are old
Our hearts are not the same

Waves of Emotion

Wading through the water
Feeling the strong pull
Swimming to the depths
Waves take control

Pushing me through the emptiness
Looking for my way
Reaching for the heavens
I begin to pray

Praying for relief
Emotions are too much
Drowning in this sadness
Because I miss your touch

Clipped Wings

My wings were clipped
A sad little bird
Stuck in a gilded cage

Not sure what to do
I reach for you
Lord heal these wings I pray

Heal these wings so I can fly
And find my way back to you

Please light my way
For your love is pure
Your love is always true

Darkness

Ice
Nightmares
Snakes
The Offer
Breadcrumbs
The Test
Classless
True Colors
The Art of Bullshit (aka empty promises)
Haunted
Darkness

Ice

The demon inside you
The devil he knows
He's frozen your heart
Turned you cold

Blue in your heart
Blue on your lips
I felt the ice
Within your kiss

The cold you radiate
From deep within your bones
I search for my way out
From all the unknows

I need to leave
before my time is through
Ending up with a cold heart
Just like you

Nightmares

You're on my mind
Playing in my head
Taking up my space

You're in my dreams
Bothering me
Nightmares start to replace

Breathing my air
Suffocation I can't bear
Choking on your lies

I'm closing you off
Building a wall
You're not allowed inside

You're trying to push through
I'm fighting with you
Keeping you on the outside

I must wake
So I can escape
The evil that you hide

Snakes

Festering under my skin
You slithered right in
A snake wrapped around my heart
Constricting you squeezed
The life out of me
You think you've been so smart

You're shedding your skin
I now see within
The evil that's in your mind
The darkness that lies
You hid deep inside
I tried to push you aside

Looking into your eyes
They're black as night
Keeping me in the dark
What you cannot see
Is deep within me
You can never take my spark

The Offer

The offer you give is empty
You say a lot of shit
You're always making promises
And going back on it

You're back and forth in your head
Overthinking is what you do
You can't seem to make up your mind
Or do what's best for you

You live in fear of being judged
Your life is wrapped in drama
More than I can deal with
But you will get your karma

Breadcrumbs

You give me just enough
Keep me hanging on
As we are going through this
Breadcrumbing me along

You say the kindest things
You always make my day
Then all the sudden
You just pulled away

You never told me why
Left me in the dark
I feel like I've been blinded
With pain in my heart

I need to find myself again
I had to pull away
Needing to heal my heart
In each and every way

The Test

I am light you are dark
I'm finally glad that I got smart
Found my strength and walked away
I will not struggle another day

You think you're a player, you have no play
Soon you will see you will get your day

You're in and out back and forth
Full of deceit you will get yours

You have everyone fooled you can't fool me
I know exactly what you'll be
Cold and empty forever alone
Growing old with the seeds you have sown

A wake-up call
You were blocked from me
This was something never meant to be

You will never find true happiness
You do not know the meaning
I feel sad for you but now I am healing

From this challenge I was given
This test I have passed
I am standing strong
I will never look back

Classless

You are classless
Bougie at best
I know you don't have
A heart in that chest

Your round and round
Like hamsters on a wheel
I don't believe you know how to feel

Your wicked ways will be repaid
Retribution will be coming your way
I only hope I see that day

Use and abuse are what you do
I could always see right through
Changes need to come to you
I don't think it's something you can do

Now that I have had my say
See you later
Make your way

True Colors

True colors are what I've seen
I had to open my eyes

True colors are what I've seen
I needed to look deep inside

True colors you hid them well
I could see right through

True colors I'm glad I did
I really don't need you

The Art of Bullshit
(aka-Empty Promises)

Lean in closer my dear
Let me whisper in your ear
All the sweet nothings I will not do
Empty promises I made to you

Empty promises made in vain
Given to you to cause you pain

Although these are things I say to you
This doesn't mean we have to do
Any of the empty promises
I made to you

Haunted

The pain you caused
Has changed me so
All for the good

The ghost you left
I have embraced
And now I'm haunting you

You see the change
And what I've become
So now the ghost is me

I'm giving you nightmares
Taking you down
Showing you who I can be

Darkness

I see into your soul
It always seems dark
You pulled on my light
You've taken my spark

You took my love and threw it away
You pull me to your darkness
I don't want to stay

I know that I have lost my way
Looking for my home
The only place that makes me feel safe
And never alone

I will find my light again
Praying for that day
I am never looking back
I will find my way

Hope And Healing

Shadows
Guarded
Changes
Lost and Found
Silver Lining
Chapters
Broken
Walls
If Only
Sunshine
Leaps of Faith
Smoke and Ashes
Lessons Learned
Rain
The Crowd
Doubt
Light of My Life
Hands of Time
Tears from Heaven
Destiny
New Paths
Parallel Lives
Wounded Soul
Hope
Paradise
Heavens Gates
Forgiveness
Faith

Shadows

Living in the shadow
Of a life that's past and gone
Will I find the strength inside
To stand up and move on

The shadows always find me
Pulling me back in
I have to fight
To find myself
Or I will fail to win

The choice is clearly up to me
To leave these shadows behind
Finding everlasting peace from destiny
Understanding this was the way
It was supposed to be

Guarded

Your devil brought you to me
My angels moved you away
They guarded over me
Could see the games you play

He fought to bring you back
But now I am too strong
My angels here are guiding me
And moving me along

Changes

Changes may be hard
Painful at times
Although they are hard
Everything will be fine

Don't let any obstacles dim your light
Know that you will always shine bright

Things need to change so you can grow
When this happens, you will know
Just what this life has in store for you
You're in your power
So just be true

Lost and Found

I found myself because of you
At a time I felt so lost
You showed me how to open up
But that came at a cost

Pain is part of life
And love is a gift

This I will cherish so
Thank you for that time with you
It was meant to help me grow

Silver Lining

Silver lining light my way
I'm in need of a better day
Days filled with happiness
Days filled with love
That can only be sent from the Lord above

Send me the guidance to find my way
Clarity I need if only for a day
That silver lining waits for me
I'm figuring out who I want to be

Seeing that silver lining lighting my way
Following it to a better day
Days filled with joy
Days filled laughter
Silver lining forever and after

Chapters

Our lives all have a story
Like chapters in a book
Pages written in destiny
Words misunderstood

We move through our lives
With all the lessons we've learned
Never knowing why
Our paths take these turns

Have we learned anything
From the choices we've made
Or are we destined
To repeat another day

Broken

Healing what's been broken
I'm waiting for the day
That you will start to realize
Just why I went away

No matter what you did
No matter what you do
You'll never be able to give me
Just what I need from you

I will heal what's been broken
Moving on with my life
Always looking to the future
Its finally looking bright

Walls

You passed this up
Although I was there
Never wanting anything but you
Too caught up in your sadness
Never knowing what to do

You came to me and I let you in
Dropping walls built up
Tearing through my blackened heart
You helped to heal it up

I've made the choice to walk away
Worrying about me
Not sure if it's the right choice
But soon I guess we'll see

It must be better than this
The sadness that never ends
Never wanting to ever lose you though
You will always be my friend

If Only

If only I had known better
If only I was told
Never felt any warmth from you
Only just the cold

Wished I pulled myself away
Before emotions grew
Wished I would have been stronger
To not end up with you

Although I wished this never happened
You did teach me a lot
Helping me find my self-worth
Putting my happiness on top

Sunshine

Sunshine in my heart
I need a new start
To cover this gaping hole

The love we once had
Had all turned bad
Why I will never know
You pulled me in
I fell hard
Never knowing what's on your mind

Over time I felt you pull away
Never were you going to stay
You were never really mine
The games you played
Were hard on me
I guess their lessons learned

I now pulled away
And look for the day
My sunshine will return

Leaps of Faith

Leaps of faith
That's what they are
Who knows what the outcome will be

Take that chance
Live that dance
All will set you free

Feel the faith that's in you
No matter what you do
Fulfilling all your dreams
You can make them all come true

Smoke and Ashes

Nothing is perfect but we can find our way
We take this life that's been given to us
Day by day

Walking through the smoke
Brushing off the ashes
Looking for the sun
We've taken our bashes

We've reached the highs
Felt the lows
Taken our time and dipped in our toes

To find the place where we belong
Finding our path
Singing our song

Lessons Learned

I've taken my hits
I was able to see
This was never meant to be

I've tried to talk
Open you up
You give nothing back to me

The happiness you give
Is for everyone else
You can't see the pain you have caused

I have lived in this darkness
Waiting on you
Putting my life on pause
Not anymore
I will find my way
Because I am so strong

I'm standing up
Healing my heart
And deciding to move on

Rain

I cannot fix you
It's too much pain
Every day it feels like rain

The gloom that hangs over
You can't see the light
I've tried to help you
Showing you that it can be bright

I'm drowning in your rain
With no hope in sight
Because you cannot be there
Because you're not right

I need to leave this place
Needing to move on
I need to save myself
And make this rain gone

The Crowd

Don't follow the crowd
Be your own person
Flourish in your own skin

You must learn how to love yourself
Before you can let love in
Once you figure that out
Your dreams will start to come true

Open your heart
To the goodness in the world
And the rest will come to you

Doubt

The waves of destiny
Flood my soul
The tides ebb in and out
Sometimes I want
To be swept away
And forget about this doubt

Though doubt is here
I'm not sure why
It pulls me back and forth
Battered and bruised
I will never lose
Faith in you my Lord

Help me push away this doubt
And all these tears I've cried
Helping me to realize true happiness
Lies deep inside

Light of My Life

Dark of night
Light of day
Haunting nightmares
Dreams of play

The sadness of this world
Happiness of life
Things we take for granted
Things we take in spite

The things that make us whole
Things that make us complete
People that we know
People that we meet

The ones who make us happy
Ones who make us sad
The ones who will stand by us
When we are feeling bad

Hands of Time

The hands of time are holding me
Bound by a ticking clock
The days tick by empty
A life I once forgot

I am looking for a way
To change my path in life
To change the emptiness I feel
In this forgotten night

This forgotten life can change
It's all up to me
To find the happiness that's there
And how good life can be

Tears from Heaven

Rain upon my skin
Feeling so cool
Tears from heaven
Bringing forth anew

Life forever changing
Watching it in awe
The wonders of this world
From something that starts so small

Finding peace in this world around me
Beauty from within
Tears that rain from heaven
To wash away our sin

Destiny

Our destiny was written in time
Scrolls of gold by the great divine

What you will do
With this life you've been given
It's your choice
Although it's been written

God has a plan
He will guide you through
Following you on your path
Until your time is through

God will take your hand
To the heavens above
He will show you what
Your life was made of

God will give you a choice
To do this again
He will walk with you
Until the end

New Paths

A new path in life
Is what I choose
I'm walking this trail
Less confused

My mind is getting clear
I'm ready for this challenge
My head held high
My karma in balance

This life is what I make of it
I have the strength inside
I'm walking on this trail
Moving along it with pride

Knowing there will be challenges
That will try to slow me down
In the end it's up to me
To find the middle ground

Parallel Lives

I see your insecurities
You see all of mine
We are like past lives
Caught up in time

Parallel lives
We have crossed many paths
Will we get this right
Or have to come back

The hands of time stop
When I'm in your arms
Then we part ways
Retreating to the dark

If we get this right
We will make it magic
No more crossing time
To make this happen

Wounded Soul

Your wounded soul calls for help
I've tried to hold you tight
I can't live in this hell with you
You're taking all my light

You always open up the door
Then slam it back on me
All the pain you hold inside
For this could never be

How do you really feel
Emotions you always hide
You never open up to me
Keep pushing me aside

Maybe this could change for us
The work starts with you
Finding your strength deep inside
Will heal your heart up too

Hope

Bringing hope is what I do
I hope this book
Will help you too

There are going to be times
When things seem dark
Just find your power
Follow your heart

Know that you can change
The things that seem bad
The rough times ahead
There's no need to be sad

They are lessons in life
That you can overcome
Have faith in these times
And the lessons you have won

Paradise

Paradise is what I had
It all got ripped away
I floated near an island
Wondering day to day

What this life might hold for me
Floating on my tears
Will I find the help I need
To pull me out of fear

You opened up my heart again
Pulled me from this abyss
You gave me what I needed
With just a simple kiss

Heavens Gates

This life has been a blessing
I've learned so very much
The beauty of this world
A loved one's special touch

Moments that fill our hearts with joy
Or can break them in two
The miracle of new life born
Sadness when it's through

The beauty of a sunset
The warmth of a dawn
The time that we have on this earth
Before we are gone

I know our time is short here
So, when my time is through
I will be at heaven's gates
There I'll wait for you

Forgiveness

Just know that I forgive you
For what you did to me
I needed to forgive you
So, I can be free

Having empathy in my heart
For what you do not know
Hoping that your time with me
I was able to help you grow

You taught me much about myself
So, I have grown form this too
I hope you find what you're looking for

That's my wish for you

Faith

I need my faith
To help me through
The darkness of these days
I kneel upon the warm ground
Then begin to pray

Lord give me strength and serenity
The power to push past
All the dark days ahead of me
That always seems to last

Lord help me turn these dark days
Into the ones of light
Help me bring an end to this
Help me win this fight

Amen

Freedom

My Demise
Ties that Bind
Control
Sounds
Toxic People
Comply
Day by Day
Soul
Your Loss
Blue
Freedom
Time
Intuition
Perfectly-Imperfect
The Wolf
The Unknown
Stronger
Imagine
Gods Rainbow
The Golden Door
Angel Wings
Walk With Me
Past
Beautiful Transformations

My Demise

Holding on to you
Will lead to my demise
I've seen all your darkness
Deep within your eyes

You tried to keep me there
You kept pulling me back
I've finally found my strength
I'm never looking back

I'm leaving you behind
Without your light to see
Leaving you in your darkness
My light is finally free

Ties That Bind

Your soul is hurting
For that I know
I've tried to help you
Your pain takes its toll

The ties that bind us
I must break
I'm pulling away
For my own sake

I hope you can find
What you're looking for
The help you need
So, you can restore

Your faith in love
Healing your broken heart
Moving on from your past
With a brand-new start

Control

You can't control me
I am too strong
Watch your back
Or you'll be gone

You can't control me
I see inside
You know it's true
You run and hide

You can't control me
I'm pushing back
So, get your bags
And start to pack

You can't control me
I'm better than that
So, make your way
And don't look back

You can't control me
You look for new prey
I only hope
They see your way

Sounds

Going through the deep woods
Trying to find my way
Hearing eerie noises
Beckoning to play

Trying to keep the dark out
Ignoring all the sounds
Sounds that forever haunt me
Trying to keep me down

I must block the sounds out
I'm looking for the sun
It's peeking through the canopy
We are becoming one

Feeling the warmth upon my skin
Pulling me through these woods
Leaving this cold world behind
Knowing that I withstood

Toxic People

Ridding toxic people
Not needed in my life
You leeched on me
Stole my energy
You are a parasite

Ridding toxic people
Did you even care
I don't believe you did
You knew I would be there

Ridding toxic people
Why you stayed I do not know
All you did was cause me pain
So now you have to go

Ridding toxic people
Finally I'm free
I'm taking back my life
And living it for me

Comply

I will not submit
I will not comply
Call it what you want
I was born to fly

With these angel wings
God has given to me
Guiding me to what
My freedoms should be

Gods love for me
Has helped me to fly
The only stamp
That will be on me
Is

I will not comply

Day by Day

I will not give power
To the things that do not serve me
It has already taken too much
Left me feeling blurry

So that I cannot see
The good that lies ahead
It leaves me with these thoughts
Swirling in my head

I will take back my power
Push the dark away
In the end
It's up to me
To go on day to day

Soul

Looking deep into my eyes
You see into my soul
You've touched my heart
Opened my mind
And make me lose control

Why am I so drawn to you
I've tried to pull away
I've tried to fight these feelings
Tried but yet I stay

I'm asking God for guidance
Asked my angels for help
I want to put this behind me
Moving on for myself

Your Loss

Your loss my gain
All you did was cause me pain
Pain that I have moved on from
Grown from this so I have won

So, take your loss and move on from me
First time in months I finally feel free
I feel sorry for you that will never be

Good riddance my dear
Wish you the best

Good luck to you and all of your mess

Blue

I've lost my way
Couldn't see the light
My path seemed dark
Full of fright

Not sure where to turn
Or what to do
Hopeless and lost
My world was blue

I pray to the heavens for guidance
I prayed to my angels for help
Needing to look deep inside
To find it for myself

Even though angels are guiding me
Walking me through life
I needed to find it for myself
To make my life feel bright

That is just what I did
Overcoming all this blue
Made my world a happy place
And you can do that too

Freedom

Freedom from this pain
I must let it go
I need to stand up
Needing to take control

Control from this pain
That has taken far too much
Looking deep inside myself
Trying to get in touch

With whom I am
And where I want to go
Feelings in my heart
That are starting to grow

I'm winning against this pain
A war that I've fought hard
Finding my new freedoms
But my heart will hold the scar

Time

The time is now past and gone
I watch the sun rising at dawn
For every minute that passes by
The sun will set, and time will fly

The hands of time will never stop
Our bodies live by a ticking clock
No one knows when the time will end
You live every day to the fullest you can

We all want to live to grow old and wise
Now that we have the time just flies
Those are years you will never get back
Always live life happy and without lack

Intuition

Stepping out of your comfort zone
Knowing who you are
Feeling you can do anything
You can go very far

This isn't always easy
Uncomfortable at the least
Only you can change your life
Don't live it by defeat

Trust your intuition
It will not steer you wrong
God blessed you with that gift
To keep you feeling strong

Perfectly-Imperfect

Perfectly- imperfect
That is what you are
Never Let anyone
Tame your bright star

No one is perfect
Just know this is true
Look deep inside
So, you can find you

When someone puts you down
Or makes you feel bad
Just know it's because
Their world is sad

Everyone is flawed
In their own unique way
You are light in this world
And will make someone's day

You are perfect

The Wolf

The wolf she lives inside me
Just beneath my skin
Wanting to come out
Beckoning from within

The darkness of the day
The brightness of the night
She's waiting on the moon
To release her of her plight

Wanting to be wild
Wanting to be free
Needing to escape this world
And what she's supposed to be

Running through the woods
Power from within
Running in the night
Releasing all her sin

The Unknown

My angels have been protecting me
Guiding me along
Although life hasn't been easy
It's made me very strong

The unknown can be scary
You have the power inside
You never know what you can achieve
Unless you go out and try

Staying loyal to yourself and who you are
Then you can reach for any bright star
Accomplish your dreams
No matter how small
Once you do that you have it all

Stronger

This is what I'm made of
I'm stronger than I think
I let this life bring me down
Push me to the brink

Days where it seems dark
Days where there is light
The ones that are happy
Or cut you like a knife

All the tests were given
To show our strength inside
I've pulled myself up
I've pulled myself out

I walk through life with pride

Imagine

Imagine who you want to be
And who you want to become

All of this will set your soul free
Finding pleasure in what you have done

Become one with God and the universe
Your angels will guide your way

Your dreams are all up to you
To live out everyday

Gods Rainbow

I have seen Gods rainbow
After the worst of the storm
A new beginning
I have been reborn

Sorrows of these dark days
Have been a test of faith
Colors from Gods rainbow
Have been my saving grace

The storm I've had to walk through
I've held my head up high
The colors I have seen
They beam down deep inside

I can accomplish anything
As long as I believe
From the colors of Gods rainbow
I'm open to receive

The Golden Door

The golden door I see it
It lies ahead of me
All I had to realize
Is that I hold the key

I will unlock this door
Leaving these sorrows behind
Tests I have been given
Will always be on my mind

My angels have always been with me
Showing me along
Guiding me to that golden door
To walk through and move on

Angel Wings

Going with the winds of change
Blowing me along
Floating on these angel wings
Like a beautiful song

Singing in my heart
Reaching to my soul
Protected by these angel wings
They help me to feel whole

Forgiving what's been done to me
Compassion from within
Knowing every battle crossed
Will be ones I won't win

Trying to find my way along
Not knowing where I'll go
Floating on these angel wings
They're helping me to grow

Protected by loved ones past and gone
They help me see my way
They blow me on these winds of change
To find a better day

Walk with me

I feel your light
It warms my soul
You walk with me everyday

When things were dark
I knew you were there
I would lean on your strength and pray

I find comfort in you
You help me through
With your power I see your light

I thank you God for being with me
And walking me through this life

Past

I have held onto the past
For far too long
I have to start letting go
I need to be strong

I will hold onto the memories
For the rest of my life
Pictures froze in time
The love
The fights

I need to move on
But I will never forget
The way you touched my life
From the first time that we met

I will see you in my dreams
When I close my eyes
Forever there with me
Until the day I die

Beautiful Transformations

Beautiful Transformations
The confusion leaving my mind
I knew that it would come to me
It just took divine time

Beautiful Transformations
I have love in my life
Never taking a day for granted
Never taking them in spite

Beautiful Transformations
This has been a long road
Mountains I've had to climb
The rivers were cold

Beautiful Transformations
I've finally found my way
The sun is shining on me
This is a better day

Beautiful Transformations
Helping others find their way
I only hope that they will find
Love and a better day

Don't miss out!

Visit the website below and you can sign up to receive emails whenever Lisa Ann publishes a new book. There's no charge and no obligation.

https://books2read.com/r/B-A-AUDBB-EFUPC

BOOKS 2 READ

Connecting independent readers to independent writers.

www.ingramcontent.com/pod-product-compliance
Lightning Source LLC
Chambersburg PA
CBHW031432130726
47989CB00003B/1109